Unlocking Hidden Compute Savings Plan Opportunities

Table of Contents

Chapter 1. Introduction

In today's digitally-driven landscape, every organization aims to leverage their computing capabilities in the most cost-effective way possible. Our Special Report titled "Unlocking Hidden Compute Savings Plan Opportunities" dives deep into this relevant subject, providing you with an invaluable roadmap to transform how you allocate your resources. This is no elusive fad; we're talking about real strategies and methodologies that lead to discernible reductions in expenditure, while bolstering your overall operations. This report does not indulge in technical jargon but promises a user-friendly discourse, packed with insights that could potentially revolutionize your cost-saving agenda. If you've been seeking that magic key to unlock the hidden treasure of compute savings, look no further - this vibrant, engaging report has been tailor-made for you! From conceptual understanding to actionable strategies, it's all here, waiting to be discovered. Let's embark on this fascinating journey together and reshape your savings plan landscape for the better.

Chapter 2. Demystifying Compute Savings Plans

Compute savings plans offer a model that allows you to save costs without compromising on the efficiency and performance of your computing systems. While these plans can be beneficial, many organizations often overlook them, mostly because of a lack of understanding or apprehension regarding their workings. In this chapter, we break down the complex world of compute savings plans, revealing their distinct features, benefits, and strategies for optimal implementation.

2.1. Introduction to Compute Savings Plans

A compute savings plan can be defined as a cost optimization strategy adopted by companies using cloud-based services. It allows you to commit to a consistent amount of compute usage (measured in $/hour) for a one-year or three-year term. The commitment is applicable across any region, thus rendering elasticity to your investments - you may switch regions or change compute families without affecting your agreement.

2.2. Compute Savings and On-Demand Instances: The Difference

The compute savings model differs from the On-Demand instance model in cloud computing. On-Demand instances mean you pay for compute capacity by per hour or per second, based on the instances you run. While this model ensures no long-term commitments, it can lead to increased costs.

On the other hand, the compute savings plan offers a discounted rate for sustained usage, allowing you to control costs better. Plus, the savings model offers greater flexibility as you can shift or transition instances within a region without altering your commitment.

2.3. Benefits of Compute Savings Plans

Compute savings plans come with various benefits that maximize the potential of your digital resources, leading to impressive cost savings.

Reduced costs:

The primary advantage of compute savings plans is that they decrease expenses significantly. By committing to a consistent usage amount, you qualify for sizeable discounts.

Greater flexibility:

The model extends the freedom to alter your instance type or CPU platform, without worrying about modifying your compute savings plan.

Increased Capacity reservations:

An optional feature, capacity reservation, enables you to reserve capacity for your instances, in a specific Availability Zone, for any duration.

2.4. Different Types of Compute Savings Plans

There are two broad types of Compute Savings Plans.

Amazon EC2 Instance Savings Plans:

These provide the maximum savings potential, up to 72%. They offer flexibility to use any size, operating system, or tenancy within a single region.

Compute Savings Plans:

These offer a discount of up to 66% and extend the flexibility across EC2 instances and AWS Fargate usage across regions.

2.5. Leveraging Compute Savings Plans

To reap the maximum benefits from compute savings plans, develop an effective strategy.

Monitor your usage patterns:

Evaluate your usage patterns and determine how much usage you want to commit to. AWS provides you with several tools to assess your usage patterns.

Optimize your investments:

Prioritize savings and flexibility to optimize your investments. For instance, if flexibility is your priority, choose the regular compute savings plan. If savings are more critical, an Amazon EC2 instance savings plan would be the better choice.

Choose length of commitment carefully:

Your commitment to a compute savings plan can either be for one or three years. A three-year plan offers more substantial savings, but it also requires a more extended commitment.

Chapter 3. Understanding Cloud Provider Pricing Models

Compute savings plans can be a game-changer when it comes to cost optimization of your digital resources. With a proper understanding and an effective strategy, you can unlock significant savings and enhance the efficiency of your computing systems. This model isn't just about saving cash; it's about creating a scalable and elastic computing environment that aligns with your business objectives and propels growth.

As we delve deeper into the ways organizations can optimize their compute resources, one critical aspect that stands out is understanding the cloud provider pricing models. Gaining knowledge about these models could be your first step towards realizing signicant savings in your organization's IT spend.

3.1. Pay-As-You-Go Pricing model

Pay-As-You-Go (PAYG) model, as the name suggests, allows users to only pay for the resources they use. This strategy eliminates upfront costs, thus making it an attractive choice for businesses.

This model is especially useful for short-term projects that might require a substantial amount of resources upfront but only for a limited period. With the PAYG model, businesses can scale up their resources when necessary and scale down when the workload is reduced. Furthermore, this model adds a layer of predictability to your IT costs, as you only pay for what you use.

However, the PAYG model might not be the most cost-effective for long-term, steady workloads. Other pricing models may offer better rates for such requirements.

3.2. Reserved Instance Pricing Model

If you have a predictable workload that will run continuously for an extended period, typically 1-3 years, a Reserved Instance (RI) pricing model can be more cost-effective than the PAYG model.

By committing to a specific usage period, you can avail of significant discounts on the standard on-demand rates. The savings can be up to 75%, particularly when you commit to more extended periods and pay for your reservation upfront.

Remember, though, that the RI model may not offer the flexibility of the PAYG model. You're committing to a fixed amount of resources for an extended period, so if your workload decreases, you may end up overpaying for unused resources.

3.3. Committed Use Contracts

Under some cloud platforms, the committed use contracts allow enterprises to commit to a certain usage for 1-3 years in exchange for significant discounts—somewhat similar to Reserved instances.

However, under Committed Use Contracts, the discounts apply not only to compute instances but also to other resources such as memory and storage. These types of contracts can be beneficial for predictable, steady-state workloads when you can estimate your resource requirements accurately over the commitment period.

3.4. Spot Instance Pricing Model

Finding economic and efficient solutions for unpredictable,

undemanding, or flexible workloads can sometimes be a challenge. That's where the Spot Instance pricing model fits in.

Spot Instances refer to unused cloud capacity that cloud providers sell at steep discounts, often up to 90% off the on-demand price. However, these are available only until that spare capacity is required by the provider, which means your Spot Instances can be interrupted and reclaimed by the provider at any point with short notice.

These instances are perfect for flexible, non-critical applications that can withstand potential interruptions. Examples include data analysis, batch jobs, testing, and development workloads.

3.5. Savings Plan

A Savings Plan offers a significant discount compared to on-demand rates in return for a commitment to consistent usage of specific resources. Unlike Reserved Instances, Savings Plans apply the discount across any set of instances you choose, irrespective of region, instance family, or size.

You agree to a usage commitment, defined in dollars per hour, and any usage up to this commitment will benefit from the reduced rates. Usage beyond your commitment will be charged at normal on-demand rates.

Understanding your workload and selecting an appropriate pricing model can lead to substantial cost savings. Combining different pricing models can often provide the best solution, and incorporating additional cost-saving strategies reviewed in this report can help maximize your savings.

Remember, cloud cost optimization is not a one-time process but requires continual monitoring and adjustment as your workload and business needs evolve.

In the subsequent sections, we'll discover how cloud services can be better measured, monitored, and managed for optimal usage and cost efficiencies.

Chapter 4. Mastering Resource Allocation and Management

The optimization of resource allocation and management is a critical component of leveraging compute savings, contributing directly to the reduction of expenditure, and fortifying operations overall. Masterful manipulation of these facets enables organizations to extract maximum value from their investment, optimizing their savings plan.

4.1. Understanding Resource Allocation

Resource allocation is the process of distributing available resources among the various entities in an organization. It involves understanding the strategic goals of the organization and determining the optimal division of resources to ensure these goals are met. Resources can be tangibly physical like hardware or intangibly virtual like software algorithms, human resource time, or network bandwidth. The underlying principle remains the same: precise application of resources where they will offer the most benefit.

Effective resource allocation is contingent on a couple of key factors. Firstly, there needs to be a clear understanding of the resources. What do they encompass? How are they applied, and what benefits are derived from their use? Secondly, there needs to be a defined strategy for their deployment. It involves planning, monitoring, and managing the resource allocation to optimize efficiency.

4.2. The Importance of Efficient Resource Management

Efficient resource management goes hand in hand with effective resource allocation. The process involves tracking, assessing, and managing the resources of an organization to guarantee that these resources are used in the most efficient manner.

With efficient resource management, organizations can anticipate possible setbacks, make informed decisions, and streamline all processes to ensure optimal performance. On a more granular level, adequate resource management can aid in avoiding resource contention, improving service quality, increasing productivity, and reducing operational costs.

4.3. Leveraging Technology for Resource Management

The advancement of technology provides us with several tools and methods to enhance resource management. High-powered tools enable us to track usage patterns, measure performance, alert resource contention, and provide automated solutions to optimize resource allocation.

Virtualization and cloud computing technologies also allow organizations to allocate and manage resources dynamically, based on the actual needs of applications. They help organizations shift from static resource allocation to dynamic resource allocation, which can significantly reduce costs, improve application performance, and enable increased flexibility.

4.4. Evaluating Resource Usage

Evaluating resource usage is a core component of resource management. This process involves tracking the consumption of resources over time, understanding usage patterns, and identifying resources that are underutilized or overutilized.

Usage data from monitoring tools can be presented in the form of reports, graphs, or dashboards which shed light on the consumption patterns and help in decision making for resource allocation. Detailed usage audits can also reveal anomalies or inefficiencies that could be rectified to optimize performance and potentially save costs.

4.5. Implementing a Resource Allocation Strategy

Implementing an effective resource allocation strategy demands a comprehensive understanding of the resources at hand and the business requirements. The strategy should be flexible enough to accommodate changing business needs and robust enough to handle sudden spikes or drops in demand.

Once a strategy is implemented, it also needs to be continually reviewed and adjusted as per the changing requirements. An effective strategy considers not just the present needs, but also anticipates future growth and changes. By doing so, the organization is not just reacting to changes, but proactively planning for them.

4.6. Conclusion

Mastering resource allocation and management plays a crucial role in unlocking hidden compute saving opportunities. It involves an understanding of your resources, efficient management, leveraging technology, evaluating resource usage, and implementing effective strategies. Organizations that hone these skills can substantially minimize their expenditures while maximizing their operational efficiency, paving the way for enhanced compute savings. Remember, the key to hidden treasure is not always a sudden insight but often the result of careful planning, reviewing, and reallocation.

Chapter 5. Exploring On-Demand vs Reserved Instances

In the ever-evolving digital milieu, the decision between On-Demand and Reserved Instances isn't straightforward. Often, businesses struggle to balance between performance requirements, budget constraints, and changing market dynamics. This chapter presents an in-depth analysis of both options, aiming to shed light on the advantages and drawbacks of each, thus aiding in informed decision-making.

Chapter 6. On-Demand Instances Explained

On-Demand Instances allow for pay-as-you-go pricing. You can rent these computing machines by the hour or by the second, depending on your needs. The flexibility and scalability inherent to this model make it a popular choice for businesses running short-term, irregular workloads that cannot be interrupted.

The prime advantage of opting for On-Demand Instances is the elimination of upfront costs. These instances are perfect for testing new applications or handling ad-hoc computing requirements. Plus, unlike single-tenancy hosting options, On-Demand Instances do not necessitate long-term commitments. This means that users have the freedom and flexibility to chop and change their instances as per their business needs.

However, these instances are costlier per hour compared to Reserved Instances. Substantial costs can accumulate if an application runs full-time for long durations. Thus, while On-Demand Instances offer unmatched flexibility and simplicity, they might not be the optimal choice for all scenarios based on budgetary considerations.

6.1. A Typical On-Demand Instance Use Case

Let's glance at a hypothetical example to underscore the utility of On-Demand Instances. Suppose a news portal with a fluctuating traffic pattern, peaking during major events and dipping otherwise. This uneven load characteristic is ideally suited to leverage On-Demand Instances. The portal can spin up additional instances during traffic surges and cull them during lulls, thus balancing performance and cost-effectively.

Chapter 7. Reserved Instances explained

Reserved Instances (RIs) provide a significant discount compared to On-Demand pricing, in exchange for a commitment to use the instance for a stipulated contractual term. These terms can range from 1 to 3 years. RIs offer a more cost-optimized solution for predictable workloads or applications that need to be online continually.

Reserved Instances can be pre-paid fully, partially, or not at all, depending on your financial constraints. Higher upfront payments lead to substantial savings over the agreement term. In contrast, no upfront payments still offer lower hourly rates than On-Demand Instances. Thus, RIs ensure a significant price advantage for long-standing applications.

Although, keep in mind, Reserved Instances are capacity reservations, a trade-off that might limit your flexibility. Consider reserved instances only if you can accurately forecast your computing needs. Sudden demand drop-offs could translate into unnecessary reservations while positive demand shocks could strain capacity.

7.1. A Typical Reserved Instance Use Case

Consider an eCommerce platform that witnesses relatively steady traffic, except during seasonal sales. The platform could save significantly by using Reserved Instances for the regular, predictable traffic, while supplementing with On-Demand Instances during sales.

Chapter 8. Making the Right Choice

There's no one-size-fits-all approach when deciding between On-Demand and Reserved Instances. Both options have their distinct pros and cons, and the right choice would largely depend on your particular use-case.

However, what if there was a way to incorporate the benefits of both, creating a versatile, hybrid approach? That's the beauty of mixing and matching said instances. An organization could reserve specific instances for predictable workloads, thereby gaining cost advantages. Concurrently, it could leverage On-Demand Instances for handling unexpected workloads. This balanced model aims at bringing together the cost-effectiveness and predictability of Reserved Instances along with the flexibility and convenience of On-Demand Instances.

Chapter 9. To Conclude

In conclusion, understanding the different compute instances is a valuable first step in unlocking hidden compute savings. The choice between On-Demand and Reserved Instances should be dictated by an in-depth understanding of your application workload nature, as well as an aligned budget strategy. By strategically selecting the right mix, organizations can drive savings while still meeting their business goals effectively. Indeed, the 'compute instance' key might be just what you need to unlock the world of savings opportunities.

Chapter 10. Shedding Light on Spot Instances

Spot instances offer a tremendous opportunity to capitalize on, particularly in groups of companies aiming to increase compute power while minimizing costs. They are unused Amazon Elastic Compute Cloud (EC2) instances available at steep reductions, usually 70-90% less than regular On-Demand pricing.

10.1. Understanding Spot Instances

There are situations where organizations find themselves in need of extra computing power, perhaps due to heavy traffic, central processing unit (CPU) intensive tasks, or sudden surges in demand. Here is where Spot Instances come into play - they allow users to procure extra processing power at a significantly lower cost than typical On-Demand instances. In effect, they're a form of computing capacity in AWS, available for less due to timing and capacity availability. When these conditions align properly, companies can utilize these instances to run their tasks at a significantly reduced price, thereby achieving computational savings.

As is the rule in any AWS EC2 instance, you pay for compute capacity per hour, but with Spot Instances, you have to bid a maximum price you are willing to pay per hour, per instance. If your bid meets or exceeds the current Spot price, your request will be fulfilled and these instances are allocated to you.

10.2. Pros and Cons of Using Spot Instances

Spot Instances are an excellent way to save money. However, they have their own set of pros and cons that must be carefully considered.

The most significant advantages of using Spot Instances include:

- Inexpensive: Spot Instances are often 70-90% cheaper than regular, On-Demand instances.

- Scalability: They allow applications to easily scale up and down based on the capacity required.

- Flexibility: Spot Instances can be utilized in a wide range of applications, including data analysis, batch jobs, background processing, and research projects.

On the other hand, the cons include:

- Unpredictability: If the Spot price exceeds your maximum bid, or if AWS requires additional capacity, your Spot Instance will be terminated with minimal notice, which may result in incomplete processes.

- Complexity: They require a deeper understanding of your applications to make the most effective use of this type of instance.

- Limited Availability: Availability depends on supply and demand for instances in the AWS marketplace, which may fluctuate.

10.3. Spot Instances vs. On-Demand and Reserved Instances

On-Demand instances are priced hourly without any upfront payment or minimum usage commitments. They're best suited for short-term, irregular workloads that cannot be interrupted.

Reserved instances are ideal for long-term workloads and offer substantial discounts when you reserve your instance for a one- or three-year term.

In contrast, Spot Instances are suitable for flexible start and end times, tasks that are feasible at massive scale, and tasks that only need to be completed when compute capacity is inexpensive - thus making it an ideal choice for cost savings, given the computations can withstand abrupt interruptions.

10.4. Spot Instance Best Practices

Effective use of Spot Instances requires a certain degree of planning and understanding which workloads are best suited for spot usage.

- Realize that not all types of workloads are suitable for Spot Instances. Applications that have hard deadlines, for instance, are not a good fit.

- Be prepared for abrupt terminations. Design your applications to be fault-tolerant and save state frequently to checkpoint work progress.

- Use Spot Fleet, a collection of Spot Instances and optionally On-Demand Instances, to launch and maintain a fleet of instances that fall within your budget.

- Implement an AWS provided mechanism to stop/hibernate instances when they are about to be interrupted.

- Consider fallback options. If Spot Instances are interrupted, consider moving the workload to On-Demand Instances until excess capacity becomes available at your bid price.

10.5. Unleashing Potential with Spot Instances

Spot Instances have tremendous potential for cost savings if employed correctly. Not only are they much less expensive than their counterparts, but they also enable a flexible compute infrastructure that scales according to demand. The possibilities with Spot Instances are intriguing, particularly for enterprises undertaking large-scale computation or those with flexible demand patterns. By understanding how you can unlock these savings opportunities by integrating Spot instances into your operations, you resultantly augment your compute power while minimizing overall costs.

Companies around the world, from startups to large enterprises, have seen substantial reductions in their AWS bills by efficiently utilizing Spot Instances. They offer an affordable way to access large scale compute power, democratizing innovation within the digital space. Spot Instances serve as a great example of how ingeniously structured, dynamic pricing models can facilitate more efficient use of resources in the digital era. In conclusion, Spot Instances are not only a cost-effective solution for flexible computation demands but also an unmistakable testament to the ongoing innovation in the digital world.

Chapter 11. Capitalizing on Compute Savings Opportunities

In today's economic climate, every penny saved is a penny earned. Ensuring cost-effectiveness in computing can often be the difference between competitive advantage and falling behind. There is no longer room for wasteful spending in the name of pursuing computational power. This requires an intelligent approach to compute savings, and three key areas form the backbone of this approach: usage optimization, pricing models, and waste reduction.

11.1. Usage Optimization

Optimizing the usage of your resources is a fundamental starting point for compute savings. Comprehensive visibility is a prerequisite to optimization. You need to know how you use your resources before you can streamline them.

A powerful way to gain this visibility is through a public cloud cost management tool. This helps monitor the efficiency of cloud resources, tracking metrics such as instance usage, demand patterns, and workload characteristics. By studying these aspects, we can derive actionable insights towards optimizing resource usage.

Understand the nature of your workloads. They could be steady, spiky, or unpredictable. Each workload type requires a unique management strategy. Not all resources need to be available 24/7. It's wasteful to pay for idle resources. With proper planning and automated scheduling, you can significantly reduce costs.

Ultimately, the benefits of usage optimization boil down to two points: increased efficiency and reduced costs. By ensuring resources are not wasted, you can allocate them to areas where they deliver the most value.

11.2. Embracing Flexible Pricing Models

Different pricing models present an excellent opportunity for compute savings. Major cloud providers offer various pricing models such as On-Demand, Reserved, and Spot Instances. Navigating these models and utilizing them to the best of your advantage can significantly reduce costs.

On-Demand models are costlier but offer maximum flexibility. They meet the needs of short-term, spiky, or unpredictable workloads.

Reserved Instances, on the other hand, are suited for predictable workloads. They offer significant savings over On-Demand, especially for long-term commitments.

Spot Instances utilize excess cloud capacity and are highly cost-effective. However, there's a risk of abrupt termination when demand surges. These are useful for flexible, interruptible tasks or for providing extra capacity when needed at a reduced price.

Each pricing model has a different use case. With a thorough understanding, you can leverage the right model at the right time, leading to significant compute savings.

11.3. Waste Reduction

Reducing waste is tantamount to creating savings. A surprising amount of IT spending goes towards maintaining outdated, unused, or underutilized resources.

Identifying such resources is the first step towards waste reduction.

A "zombie" virtual machine, for instance, could be eating into your budget. Periodically reviewing your infrastructure for such redundancies can help reduce waste.

Ineffective scaling also leads to considerable wastage. Over-provisioning stems from the fear of underperformance—but in the cloud, scaling is flexible. An infrastructure right-sized to your needs ensures you pay for what you use, creating huge savings.

Remember, waste reduction is not a one-off task; it's an ongoing process. Regularly monitor and adjust your infrastructure to prevent waste from creeping back in.

In conclusion, the techniques covered here are just an overview of the transformative methods available to transform how you view compute savings. Use them as a starting point to adapt a more intelligent and strategic approach towards your resources. By incorporating these practices, you can redefine your savings plan and create a landscape that benefits everyone in your organization. Every dollar you save is another dollar you can invest back into your operations to drive growth. Adoption may seem challenging initially, but the benefits far outweigh the initial hurdles. It's time to seize these opportunities, make the shift, and let cost savings fuel your future growth.

Chapter 12. Innovative Use Cases of Compute Saving Plans

Every organization striving for technological innovation is looking for more cost-effective methods to utilize their computing capabilities. Harnessing these computational resources efficiently allows organizations to create innovative solutions and services. Efficiency, in the context of compute resources, is often a matter left unexplored, but immense potential lies in uncovering these hidden opportunities.

12.1. Leveraging Elasticity for Compute Savings

One of the core principles that enable organizations to innovate in terms of cost savings is the idea of leveraging "elasticity." The elasticity of cloud computing implies that resources are not finite, rigid blocks, but flexible entities that can be altered to suit the needs of the moment.

The modern-day application landscape is dynamic, experiencing peaks and valleys in traffic that necessitate a flexible resource allocation strategy. Static resource provisioning, where resources are constant regardless of traffic, is inefficient and often expensive. Leveraging the elasticity of cloud computing allows companies to match their resource allocation to their traffic patterns and save indirectly on costs.

Consider a retailer with an e-commerce website. Its traffic is erratic, experiencing high traffic during the holiday season and sales, but relatively low traffic during other periods. By monitoring trends and implementing an elastic resource provisioning strategy, the retailer can provision more resources during high traffic to maintain performance and fewer resources during low traffic periods. This alignment not only helps maintain optimal performance but also reduces expenses.

It's noteworthy to mention that the cost savings don't always stem from the resources but also from the reduced need for operations personnel to constantly monitor and adjust resources.

12.2. Optimizing Reserved Instances and Savings Plans

Another innovative approach to reduce the cost of compute resources is optimizing the use of Reserved Instances (RIs) and Savings Plans. These are offerings that various cloud providers, like AWS, offer at a lower cost to users who commit to using a certain volume of resources for a longer term.

By carefully analyzing workloads, organizations can determine which resources are steady and require a long-term commitment. Transferring these steady workloads to Reserved Instances or Commitment Plans results in guaranteed performance at reduced costs. The savings achieved by these plans can then be used to fuel investments in other innovative projects.

12.3. Cost Savings through Automation and Scheduling

Automation is a significant game-changer in the tech world, and this fact holds in the sphere of compute savings too. Scheduling and automation tools can help to define start and stop times for different resources based on business hours or peak usage times.

When workloads do not need to run 24/7, scheduling offers a simple and effective method to cut down costs. For example, development and testing environments only need to be active during business hours. They can be turned off during non-working hours to save on costs. By scheduling the start and stop times of such non-production environments, organizations can ensure an efficient use of compute resources.

Automation platforms can also leverage machine learning algorithms to predict traffic patterns, enabling a smarter allocation of resources. This predictive provisioning can further optimize costs by pre-emptively allocating resources and preventing unnecessary scaling.

12.4. Exploration of Spot Instances

Spot Instances serve as another excellent avenue for cost savings. These are surplus resources that cloud service providers auction off at significantly lower prices. Organizations with flexible workloads can take advantage of these discounted resources.

However, spot instances come with their own unique constraints - they can be terminated by the provider at short notice when the demand for the resources grows. Therefore, using spot instances, while very cost-effective, requires careful planning and management.

Example use-cases include batch processing jobs that can handle interruptions, scientific research, or any job that can leverage the high-throughput computing provided by spot instances.

An organization might have certain tasks or jobs that are time-insensitive but computationally intensive. Using expensive on-demand resources for such jobs might not be necessary. Spot instances come in as a cost-effective solution in such scenarios.

12.5. Conclusion

The strategies presented in this discussion provide diversified and innovative approaches in the paradigm of compute savings. By judiciously embracing a mix of these strategies aligned with their individual use-cases, organizations can overhaul their compute costs and unlock hidden opportunities for cost savings.

Highlighting the versatility of cloud computing, strategies like leveraging elasticity, optimizing Reserved Instances and Commitment Plans, using automation and scheduling, and exploring Spot Instances can guide an organization along the path of efficient resource utilization and, in turn, substantial cost savings.

Each unique operational scenario requires a unique mix of these strategies. The mantra to unlocking these hidden compute savings lies in understanding the organization's specific needs and designing a strategy that catifies those needs while providing innovative and effective compute savings. The potential for cost-cutting and efficiency is there, waiting to be unlocked and harnessed.

Understanding this potential, and the strategies through which it can be realised, are essential first steps in the right direction for all organizations looking to gain an edge in today's cut-throat business environment.

Chapter 13. Analyzing Total Cost Ownership in Cloud Computing

Total Cost of Ownership or TCO is a comprehensive assessment of IT spending that entails a methodical review of all costs associated with an investment. In the context of cloud computing, it includes direct and indirect costs throughout the lifecycle of the cloud environment; ranging from the procurement and management expenses to training costs, maintenance, and infrastructure - all with a keen view towards determining a firm's Return on Investment (ROI).

13.1. Demystifying TCO

Though often glossed over, understanding TCO holistically is pivotal to optimizing your IT expenditure. It's not just about how much you pay for the cloud service upfront; it's also about indirect costs derived from its use, alongside costs associated with potential downtime or disruptions. The TCO depends largely on the service model you opt for: Infrastructure as a Service (IaaS), Platform as a Service (PaaS), or Software as a Service (SaaS). Each brings a distinct costing structure and a unique set of variables that impact the overall TCO.

13.2. Service Models and Their Impact On TCO

Service Model	Characteristics	Cost Considerations
IaaS	Provides virtualized computing resources over the Internet	Pricing depends on the consumption of resources (memory, processing, storage, and network)
PaaS	Provides a platform that includes an operating system, a programming language execution environment, a database, and a web server	Pricing is often based on the number of users or the size of the deployed applications
SaaS	Delivers applications over the Internet on a subscription fee model	Pricing usually includes costs associated with licensing, support, and fees for usage

13.3. On-premise versus Cloud TCO

The evaluation of your TCO should also consider your current IT infrastructure cost; this often entails a comparison between on-premise and cloud solutions. On-premise solutions involve upfront costs (CAPEX), including servers, network equipment, storage, and facilities to house the equipment. There are also ongoing costs including staff to maintain and support the hardware, licenses, energy, and periodic updates or replacements for hardware.

In contrast, the cloud model involves predictable ongoing costs (OPEX). With its pay-as-you-go model, it empowers businesses to scale services according to their need, only when they need it. Not only does cloud computing significantly reduce the initial investment, but it also reduces the burden of ongoing maintenance and support, supplying more monetary savings.

13.4. Factoring in Indirect Costs

While direct costs are relatively straightforward, there are several indirect costs that should be factored into the TCO. These include:

1. Cost of downtime, system data breaches, loss of productivity due to system inconsistencies

2. Opportunity costs, including time taken to manage on-premise infrastructure that could be otherwise used to focus on core business functions

3. Training and development costs for the IT teams to manage the existing or new solution

4. Costs linked with compliance and audits, especially when using on-premise solutions

5. Costs associated with software and hardware obsolescence

It's worth noting these costs are less predictable and often overlooked, but they do have a significant impact on the TCO.

13.5. Calculating Total Cost of Ownership in Cloud Computing

The Total Cost of Ownership in Cloud Computing can be calculated using the following formula:

TCO = Direct Costs + Indirect Costs

To quantify direct costs, simply add the expenses related to the acquisition, implementation, and maintenance of the service. Indirect costs, however, are trickier due to their elusive nature. They mostly depend on estimations and averages, reconciling tangible figures with factors like the cost of downtime or opportunity costs.

13.6. Lowering TCO with Cloud Adoption

The economic benefit is one of the primary reasons businesses migrate to the cloud. Studies have shown that on average, organizations see a TCO reduction of about 50% over a three-year period after moving to the cloud.

Beyond the hardware and support costs eliminated by cloud adoption, scalability is another huge benefit. With traditional, on-premise IT services, organizations often overbuild their infrastructure to prepare for potential future needs. In the cloud, businesses only need to pay for what they use, providing the flexibility to scale up or down as demand changes.

13.7. Conclusion

Every investment demands a thorough review of its cost and return potential. TCO provides such an understanding for organizations exploring cloud computing, incorporating both direct and indirect costs to provide comprehensive insights. By fully realizing the capabilities of cloud computing while understanding the potential pitfalls, organizations can find the optimal balance, resulting in a TCO that validates a move to the cloud and increases ROI. Purchasers and decision-makers are urged to undertake a meticulous study of TCO when considering their cloud investments, paving the way for a financially productive and technologically robust organization of the future.

Chapter 14. Strategies for Efficient Financial Forecasting

A robust financial forecast is a fundamental tool for every organization. The procedural steps involved play a crucial role in guiding businesses to cost-effective success. It can help identify the unseen potential of compute saving plans and enable financial leaders to make informed decisions that will pave the path to better operational efficiency.

14.1. Understanding the Importance of Financial Forecasting

Financial forecasting is today a critical activity that allows organizations to estimate future financial outcomes on their current operational and financial standings. The objective is to make well-informed, efficient resource allocation decisions. A cogent financial forecast can highlight the likelihood of a profitable future, one where the organization holds sway over its operational spend to a large extent. It can spell the difference between pell-mell spending and concrete saving plans.

Such robust predictions hinge on a deep understanding of the organization's revenue and cost patterns. Casting an eye into the future of finances allows you to grasp the financial flow, pointing out areas where you can potentially lever your compute savings. Stepping up forecasting competitions calls for a comprehensive understanding of the major drivers impacting your financial performance.

14.2. Rethinking Revenue Forecasting

In every organization, revenue is a core driver of financial performance. Revenue forecasting, therefore, is a significant component of the financial forecasting model. An effective revenue forecasting process can help you understand your market's dynamics, customers, new opportunities, and the competitive landscape—all critical components of compute saving opportunities.

Revenue forecasting practices typically involve the following:

1. Evaluating your business' historical performance.

2. Understanding customer behaviors and market trends.

3. Analyzing the past and current performance of your products or services.

4. Identifying potential opportunities for your business in the future.

But, it's not just about these practices - efficiency comes into play when you calibrate your methods and strategies to align with your specific needs, particularly in your quest for compute savings. Advanced data analytics models can play a vital role here, helping your organization delve deeper into micro trends that can inch you closer to your savings goals.

14.3. Using Cost Forecasting Techniques

Cost forecasting is just as critical as revenue forecasting, and perhaps more so when it comes to uncovering compute saving opportunities. Reasonable cost prediction can enable businesses to identify potential savings, reduce unnecessary expenditure, and improve profitability.

The process should hinge on these basic principles:

1. Understanding your overall expenditures.

2. Examining historical cost data.

3. Forecasting future sector trends.

4. Assessing the effectiveness of the current cost-saving measures.

Adding a layer of efficiency here implies being futuristic in your approach. It's about bringing into the picture innovative measures that can add to your cost savings. This calls for intelligent use of technologies such as artificial intelligence (AI) and machine learning (ML), which can analyze large data sets to predict future costs accurately.

14.4. Optimizing Resource Allocation

Understand that resource allocation is a two-pronged journey – it's about maximizing gains while minimizing losses. The primary objective, invariably, is to minimize expenditure and allocate computing resources wisely to impact cost-efficiency positively.

Building an efficient resource allocation mechanism involves the following:

1. Taking into account every resource at your organization's disposal.

2. Understanding and prioritizing individual project requirements.

3. Using real-time data to inform your decision-making.

4. Consistently updating and fine-tuning your allocation strategies to achieve optimal results.

With this, the efficiency factor keeps looping back to using advanced technologies to understand and illustrate the big picture. Real-time data powered by AI can provide insights into your current resource use, and machine learning can draw out patterns that indicate whether you're on the right track regarding your compute savings.

14.5. Embracing the Right Technologies

Clearly, technology has an important role to play in efficient financial forecasting. Cutting-edge tools such as AI and ML can enhance the accuracy and efficiency of forecasts significantly, yielding compute savings in the process.

Organizations must continuously evaluate emerging technologies and invest in those that promise to bolster their efforts in efficient financial planning. In many cases, businesses may need to overhaul their legacy systems or at least integrate newer technologies into their current infrastructures to remain competitive and cost-efficient.

Data platforms, AI algorithms, and automation tools can together create an ecosystem that enables streamlined financial forecasting and aids in significant cost savings. It's not about the grandeur of the tools you employ – it's about their alignment with your specific needs and goals.

14.6. Optimizing Processes and Training Teams

For any strategy to work effectively, it's crucial to focus on process optimization and seamless implementation. Automating repetitive tasks, streamlining workflow, and enhancing the skill set of the workforce can make a noticeable difference.

Digital transformation isn't just about adopting the right tools but also about tailoring processes to suit the newly integrated technologies. It's equally important to train the workforce to handle the new systems and adopt a 'tech-first' mindset.

At this juncture, it's paramount to create a balance between man and machine - embrace advancements, but also invest in human skills that bolster these advancements. It will not only streamline your operations but also enable your organization to uncover and leverage compute savings plan opportunities.

Financial forecasting can propel your cost-saving plan from a mere prospect to a reality, allowing you to sail smoothly even in choppy economic waters. It's time to adopt these strategies for efficient financial forecasting, freeing up more resources for investments that drive your organization's growth.

Chapter 15. Practical Steps to Implement Your Compute Savings Plan

Starting to implement a Compute Savings Plan? Then you're in the right place. This portion will walk you through all the practical steps and considerations you should be taking note of to make the most out of your journey toward enhanced computing efficiency.

Chapter 16. Initial Assessment

The first step should always be to conduct a comprehensive assessment of your compute environment: * Establish an inventory of your existing compute resources. Keep a record of the specifications, capacities, and utilization rates of your hardware and software assets. * Get a snapshot of your existing operations. You need to identify bottlenecks and inefficiencies in your current workflow. * Document the roles and responsibilities of all stakeholders. This will help clearly define who needs to be involved in the savings plan and implementation. * Understand your financial factors. Determine your current running costs, wastage costs, cost per workload, and overall return-on-investment (ROI).

Chapter 17. Planning Your Initiative

Based on your initial assessment, you can now start planning your compute savings strategy.

- Establish your objectives: What are your business goals? How can the compute savings initiative support them?

- Choose a framework: There are plenty of frameworks available to guide your initiative. These could be lean, six sigma, or others.

- Define key performance indicators (KPIs): Use your objectives to set appropriate targets and benchmarks.

- Develop your plan: Include step-by-step instructions, schedules, and assign responsibilities.

- Consider risks: What roadblocks might you encounter during your initiative? Develop preventive measures and contingency plans.

Chapter 18. Executive Buy-in and Support

Successful implementation of your compute savings strategy usually requires the full backing of your executive team. Achieving this may entail:

- Educate executives on the benefits: Use case studies and/or ROI projections to show the benefits of optimizing your compute environment in line with business outcomes.

- Align the initiative with business strategy: Show how the savings plan aligns with broader strategic initiatives.

- Set expectations: Crucial to securing executive buy-in is setting realistic expectations and highlighting that savings will come over time, not immediately.

- Create a communication plan: Regular updates about each step's progress and achieved benefits can strengthen support and commitment.

Chapter 19. Implementation Strategy

Once you have your plan and the necessary support, you can start implementing your savings plan. To ensure a successful outcome, consider the following:

- Start small and scale up: Testing your strategies on a smaller scale before full implementation can help identify potential obstacles and solutions.

- Encourage adoption: Concerted efforts to engage everyone in the savings initiative are critical to its success.

- Regularly track progress: Regular progress reports against your KPIs will show if your plan is achieving its intended objectives or needs to be adapted.

Chapter 20. Review and Iterate

The last of these practical steps is to review and iterate on your plan. Your first implementation might not be perfect, so regular reviews are important.

- Hold review meetings: These should include all stakeholders and be held regularly to track progress and discuss any issues.

- Analyze your results: The primary aim of these meetings will be to compare actual results against your KPIs.

- Identify improvements: Where progress falls short, work together to identify improvements or alternatives.

- Iterate your plan: Incorporate your learnings into an updated plan for the next iteration of your savings initiative.

This detailed roadmap serves as a general guideline and naturally, everyone's computing landscape and business needs may differ. Hence, be prepared to adapt and revise as the needs of your organization evolve. Consistently aiming for improvement and adapting to shifting conditions, you're maneuvering your organization into a position of cost-effective and efficient computing. One last piece of advice? Don't be afraid to think outside the box. Unconventional strategies could potentially offer the greatest rewards.